I dedicate this book to those who continue to stick by me,
to those my previous book has helped,
and to those whose love I cannot be without.

Thank you.

A million times, thank you

Contents

Foreword

Hi dear reader,

Thank you for picking up this little book of mindfulness.

Life is a complex journey. Each turn is an experience full
of lessons, those that we learn from, those that hurt us, and
those that leave us with a smile.

What mindfulness seeks to do is provide you with a single
moment of peace, of silence, of ease.

What this book seeks to do is provide you with tools that I
myself have learnt and used when I've needed this peace,
which will hopefully give you the peace you truly deserve.

To feel overwhelmed? That's okay.

To understand how to tackle it? Let's go through it together.

I've got you.

Turn the page, and let's begin.

Sofia A

x

Choose You

Chasing gratification through a notification

Chasing validation for anonymous reciprocation

Choosing material, missing the ethereal

Your mask, a face, the public lace

Burying sounds from inner child bounds

Restricting the free, not allowing to be

Hold wait, for a moment, make room for atonement

Choose now your best, we don't second guess

Choose authenticity, you are not your sensitivity

Check in, it's you, such power coming through

Take the hand of the higher, it is all you require

Be aware of doubt, then split, go without

Importance comes in what others don't see

For this time around, I choose only me

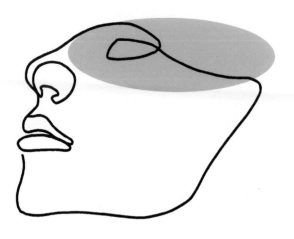

Know

Waking from slumber
To the hearts' ongoing thunder

Can be a frightening tale

A build up of woes
Or troublesome foes

Can lead ones doubt to fail

Quick changes however
From the route altogether

Is something quite powerful within

Remembering they care
And knowing they are there

Will aid your energy wearing thin

You are stronger than before
Your body is so much more

I'm so proud of what you have to show

Let's take a deep breath
And alleviate your stress

You are loved far more than you know

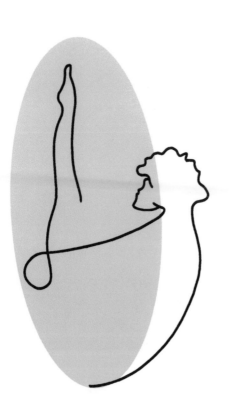

Know

It sounds simple
Doesn't it
Time for yourself

But what many don't do
Is drop the clock
For their health

Names they vary
Hygge, self care

But what it all comes down to
Is that you're here
Not there

A hot drink
A bath
Your favourite book

It's a moment for contentment
You just see
Don't look

No intention
Just still
No effort is there
All but Simple,
Unconscious will

Begin

At the beginning of mindfulness is realisation
The need to feel peace without demonstration
What you might not know is the open possibilities
And that, within you, you already have the facilities

Perhaps

Perhaps we didn't realise
How much we were truly loved

Perhaps they didn't tell us
Until push came to shove

Perhaps we needed more
Yet lost our own validation

Perhaps unclear expectations
Caused fault in reciprocation

Perhaps they did mean well
And what we thought was not the case

Perhaps love is simply complex
And is not something we chase

Perhaps we take our bias
Which chooses only the cold

Perhaps we move forward
And accept that we're brave and bold

Perhaps it is a learning
Ones comments translated to pain

Perhaps we take this notion
And never we listen again

Perhaps we now take moments
Choose peace instead of want, of fear

Perhaps you validate your own strength
For you are quite incredible, my dear

Take My Hand

Hello my child
Hi, how are you?

Are you bound by life's mysteries
Some odd, some true?

What fray sits within
How about we explore?

I know, you know
That you mean so much more

Take my hand
Follow my steps

I promise it's worth it,
There's someone you've met

They've been there all along!
In your heart, your soul

You must welcome them in
Align your life's goal

They speak not of ego
They accept good with bad

I promise if you speak
Your soul shall be glad

Stand before this mirror
Look into your eyes

Reach out your hand
Drop construct and lies

I am your conscious
Your higher self

You are ready now to meet me
In sickness and in health

Welcome my child
Please, take my hand

It is time for peace
For purpose, as planned

Life begins now
In this moment, you see

With love, with gratitude
My higher self is me

Morning

Waking up
Gathering sun rise

No rush
Sit for a minute

Close your eyes

Take 10
Take a moment

Before starting the day

Gratitude comes to play

Precious moments
Are these

So sit

Take heed

Forgive and Forget

To forgive is to let go
To what is stressing you so
Does it matter, will it ease
Tell me lovely, please

For I know not of holding
To tag on to scolding
That will take pressure away
No matter what you say

So forgive, and forget
Love and accept
For the pain of seeking solace
Will be a stranger unmet

Senses

Come to a stop.

Hear the breeze
Close your eyes
Feel at ease

Take a breath.

Take in the air
Feel at peace
All is fair

Drop your shoulders.

Listen, don't try
Relax your stomach
A positive sigh

Use your senses.

Make light of feel
Separate yourself
Use senses to heal

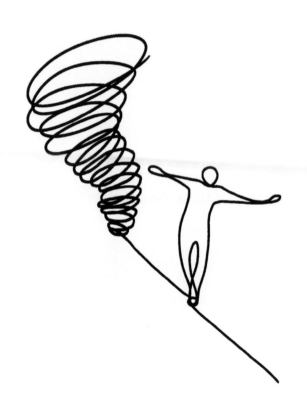

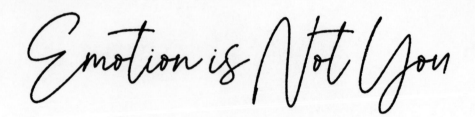

Emotion is Not You

When life proves emotional
When life proves hard

Bring yourself back to this very moment

You are not your anxiety
You are not your emotion

Come back to now, for it is all we have

A deep breathe in, hold
A deep breathe out

You've got this sweet child, now onwards

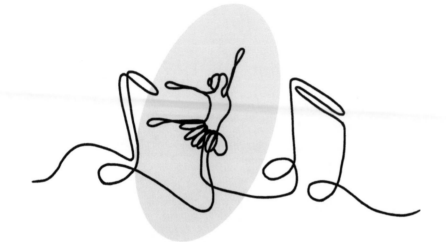

Your Favourite Song

Notable notes
With emotive quotes

Will connect with your emotion

What music can gather
Impacts the latter

Avoiding anxious commotion

No matter the connotation
Listen with elation

Turn it up, my child, relax

Whatever the genre
Feel it for longer

Enjoy semantics and syntax

Good for the soul
Meditation or goal

A chord to help you feel strong

Turn off the outside
Nurture the inside

And switch on your favourite song

Once More

Through darkness comes light
Deepest pain gives relief

Your process is now
Give love, forgive yourself

Fluidity in feeling
Is part of sonder

And now, you can breathe
You've seen it through, once more

Conversations With Yourself

How do you speak to you?
Is it something that you do?

How do you feel today?
Do you answer, I'm okay?

How does your voice sound?
By what light are you bound?

Is it positivity you spread?
Or existential dread?

The conversations within
Are they wearing thin?

Do you say I love you?
With affirmation shining through?

If not, why not?
Muster all that you've got

Does your inner child know,
That you love it so?

Look in to the mirror
See yourself clearer

Speak to your soul
Let the tongue roll

Say it loudly with me
Give love with glee

If it takes some time
Baby steps, are fine

Perhaps a word a day
So that come what may

Self love shall be met
And don't ever forget

Conversations with yourself
Are not left on the shelf

One Breath

When life gets too much
One breath provides the crutch

If all around seems manic
One breath alleviates panic

If he said something untoward
One breath cuts that cord

Breathe in, breathe out
In through the nose; out of the mouth

Deep breath for the soul
Deep breaths to feel whole

One breath, all in
One breath to begin

You are strength, you know
One breath, let's go

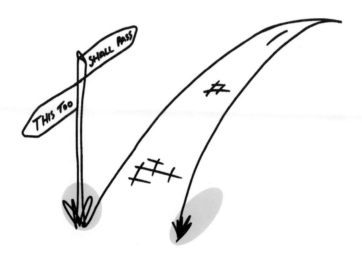

What Once Was

For a change will come
And so, it will go

Speak not of transition
But honour it so

What acceptance is nigh
Must come to light

For what once was
Has passed, like the night

Purpose Or Pity

Yet what we are about to discover
Is that life's complexities serve a learning path

The path of purpose vs pity

We know that life goes on and that it meanders
Often not freely so, but intentionally

Remind your soul of the power of choice
Take the road of the higher self and choose, not chance

Accept uncertainty for opportunity
What it is, what has happened, does not determine who you are

Life's uncertainties are expected, we know this
Yet the problems become problems when we make it so

Listen to yourself, understand your reaction
Process and heal, but do not put down life's book

Read it, create it, and know that all characters are part of your
incredible story

Thank life for the lessons it has given you
Stand tall in gratitude, kindness and savouring

Shall we sit and sigh or look only to the dark
Or must we accept that without dark, there is no light

Life becomes then a room of glorious cracks
This lack of perfection shows only character

Take your knowledge, each morsel of the bad and the good

You have a choice right now, a decision to make

Purpose, or pity?

Change. We Accept

It isn't the finale
That needs your concern
It's only the process
The twist the turn

Don't wait for the end
The beginning or start
For it is only the middle
That needs peace from your heart

Only now is what we have
Accept good and bad
Pave the way for change
Make friends, sweet nomad

There is no ending
Only an ongoing path
Something little each day
Will save you from wrath

For if you look to the future
With avoidance of now
Lack of peace with change
Will depress your brow

Emotion from the soul
Is better placed in process
Not the finale of goal
That one seems to undress

Remove concept of time
Of structure and plan
Understand that change

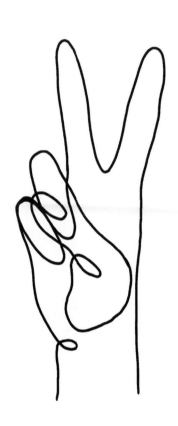

Only Today

The complexity of today
Will only be a memory, soon

Realise now is all you have
Before giving your emotion to tomorrow

Turn the spotlight on to the present
Choose self love, take it slow

Comfort amongst other emotions
May or may not be continuous

Know that right here will come and go
No matter how different the show

Love That Matters

The love that matters most today and all other days, is self love

For self love, is the beginning and the source of all other loves we hold in our life

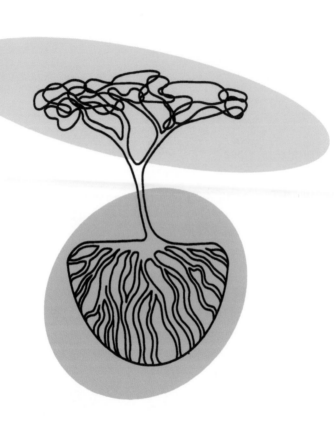

Lay

Let go of your gender

Let go of your role

Drop your name

Breathe

In through the nose

And out through the mouth

Only breath
Only flow

Who are you now?

After the drop; comes you, comes truth

Welcome to awakening

Lay down

Realise my child

That you are in the world,

but not of it

Open

Stay open to life's lessons
From friends family and foe

To close off the world and
Cut from it your hearing is a dangerous way to go

Stay open to your intuition
To your inner soul and being

For ignoring who you truly are
Brings pain and lack of seeing

Stay open my sweet child
To the complex world we live in

We are one, we don't know
And intelligence is adaptation for the driven

Friendship

Pick up the phone
I promise it's worth it

They love you
They cherish you

More than you could ever know

Tell them how you're feeling
Tell them
Let it out
Be at peace

You've got this

Walls to Build

Pick which wall to build my love
The grain, the stick, the colour

Choose which path to take my love
For peace, not pain to smother

Pick which wall to build my love
Whether protection or defence

Choose which path is righteous
Not those which leave you tense

But what you must understand my love
Is that now is yours to keep

Pick which wall to build my love
For one must let them in

Build boundaries over fences
Build walls for strength and power

Choose openness and accept risk
To avoid a life of sin

But do not build those which fail you
Those which keep you sour

I know they broke you, hurt you
I know the scar runs deep

Choose not the walls of bitterness
But those of love and care

For a wall too high, to a passerby
Might only show you're not there

Let in the love, be open to relations
Accept nothing is easy, bask in patience

You cannot fix the hurt as much as you do wish it so
So let the light shine from you, for your walls my love, they glow

Guidance

Perhaps they will not change
Perhaps you're older now
Perhaps a different generation
Will cause a sweaty brow

Perhaps they say the worst
When what they want is the best
Perhaps you need a deep breathe
Before getting it off your chest

Perhaps you walk away now
From childhood dreams and fears
Perhaps you accept processing
The hurt from all these years

Perhaps you have the tools you need
Within your wonderful soul
Perhaps it's time to open the box
Before life truly takes its toll

Perhaps this is your first step
Towards acceptance love and light
Perhaps this is simply a lesson
Know that the past is no longer in sight

Perhaps it is time my child
For you and love to connect
Perhaps give positivity and confidence
Self love care and respect

For once you show yourself what's real
What's truly deserved and there
You'll reap the benefits for you and others
Perhaps show the mirror, you care

Temporary

This is temporary, you know

You

Be unapologetic
Be bold
Be brave
Be confident

For who else is there, who matches the divine you

Stay high
Stay young
Stay happy
Stay mindful

For what else is there, which matches your energy

For you
For here
For now
For forever

For there is no when, but only this very moment

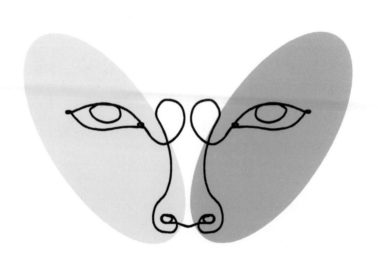

Perspective

You see the world through just one lens
Your eyes, your experience, life is written with a different pen

We are one as a whole yet different in history
Yet what stands in importance is not yesterday's mystery

Give thanks for the life you've been made to wonder
And accept, saviour and admire the sonder

Nobody really knows what to expect
Which makes life so beautiful, unique, perfect

The camera you own is only yours to see
Others have images that differ to you and me

Know that perspective is affected by experience and such
Do not be fooled by assumption and touch

If they are saddened, look to teach, do not stand and preach
For the mind of one being has only one seat

Let us share our souls, our minds, our play
For all we really have is only today

Do not waste it telling others how to have a good time
Know that it isn't only you with a thought, a mind

Different lenses, but only one love
For love is the purpose, both below and above

Timeless

It is not that there is no time, it is that there is no time

For time is simply a construct, and to think of yesterday and tomorrow

Is one sure way to forget about what we truly have, which is now

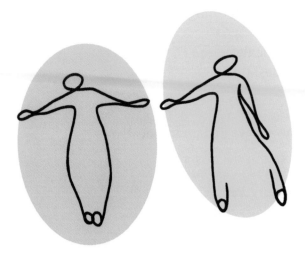

Detach

Did they walk, or did they stay?
It should not matter, either way

But the relationship was strong?
Yes, but I shan't hold for long

Can you not feel heavy pain?
From it, I must destain

Did their words knock you down?
Only a moment was wasted on frown

Did they say sorry, so you can live?
All I must do, is forgive

So you simply breathe and let go?
Release, is all we must know

One

Perception is deterministic
Of billions of lives, not so simplistic

I wonder if we could stop to see
The complex world that is you and me

For we are as one, them and I
Not one but many, pass us by

Beautiful parts of the same breath
There is no finite, no life and death

Us and we, a collective, a whole
Only love is the food which must fill our bowl

Kindness

Perhaps today
Is one of those days
Where you treat yourself
In the kindest way

Lack of sleep
A bicker, a frown
Can leave you feeling
Upside down

Let yourself choose
Your favourite treat
Ring a dear friend
Get something to eat

For know tough days
However bad and slow
Your body and mind
Need you, you know?

Printed in Great Britain
by Amazon

18303051R00038